Learn to Say No!

Inhalants

Angela Royston

Heinemann Library
Chicago, Illinois

Designed by AMR
Illustrations by Art Construction
Originated by Ambassador
Printed in Hong Kong

04 03 02 01 00
10 9 8 7 6 5 4 3 2 1

Royston, Angela.
    Inhalants / Angela Royston.
        p. cm. – (Learn to say no!)
    Includes bibliographical references and index.
    Summary: Discusses some of the substances that are abused by inhaling
them, the effects of solvents on the body, and how to avoid the dangers
involved in solvent abuse.
    ISBN 1-57572-237-2 (library binding)
    1. Solvent abuse—Juvenile literature. 2. Solvents—Health aspects—Juvenile
literature. 3. Substance abuse—Prevention—Juvenile literature. [1. Solvent
abuse. 2. Substance abuse.] I. Title.

HV5822.S65 R69 2000
362.29'9—dc21   99-088154

Acknowledgments
The Publishers would like to thank the following for permission to reproduce
photographs: Chris Honeywell, p.5; David Walker, pp.20, 23; Eye Ubiquitous,
p.21; Gareth Boden, pp.4, 28; Image Bank, pp.13, 18; John Cleare, p.29;
PhotoEdit/David Young-Wolff, p. 17; Popperfoto, p.8; Sally & Richard Greenhill,
p.22; Stock Boston/Chuck Pefley, p. 14; Telegraph Colour Library, p.19; Tony
Stone, pp.6, 26, 27; Trip, p.25

Cover photograph reproduced with permission of Gareth Boden

Special thanks to Pam Richards for her comments in the preparation of this
book.

Every effort has been made to contact copyright holders of any material
reproduced in this book. Any omissions will be rectified in subsequent
printings if notice is given to the Publisher.

Some words in this book are in bold, **like this.** You can find out what they
mean by looking in the glossary.

Contents

What Are Drugs? 4

What Are Inhalants?. 6

Inhalant Use and the Law. 8

Effects on the Body 10

Effects on the Mind 12

Regular Sniffing. 14

Danger! 16

Why Do Some People Do It?. 18

Giving Up. 20

Saying No. 22

Avoiding Difficult Situations 24

Dealing with Stress 26

Preventing Inhalant Abuse 28

Useful Contacts 30

More Books to Read. 30

Glossary 31

Index 32

What Are Drugs?

A drug is any substance that affects your body and changes the way you feel. There are three groups of drugs—**medicines**, **legal drugs,** and **illegal drugs**.

Medicines
Many medicines, such as cough medicines and painkillers, help to soothe the symptoms of a disease. Other medicines, such as antiseptic cream and antibiotics, tackle the disease itself. Some medicines can only be **prescribed** by doctors, but over-the-counter medication can be bought at a drugstore or supermarket.

Legal or illegal?
Legal drugs include medicines, but the term usually refers to drugs, such as alcohol and tobacco. These drugs affect the way a person feels, but they are not illegal for adults. Tea, coffee, and cola are legal drugs, too. Illegal drugs include **marijuana**, **heroin**, **Ecstasy**, and **LSD** and are forbidden by law.

People who suffer from asthma sometimes need medicine to help them breathe more easily. The drug may be taken as a tablet or breathed in from a spray.

Inhalant Abuse

This book will tell you about inhalant abuse called **sniffing** or **huffing**. The substances that people inhale are common products, such as glue, gasoline, and lighter fluid. They are not dangerous when used in the way they are intended to be used, but when sniffed, they are deadly **chemicals**.

Many drugs are legal, including tea and coffee. And many legal household products are very dangerous when misused.

Did you know?

When a chemical is inhaled, it can be a dangerous **hallucinogen**. A hallucinogen alters the way a person sees or hears things. Apart from medicines, most drugs are either **stimulants**, **depressants**, or hallucinogens. A stimulant, such as caffeine in cola and coffee, makes your body work faster. A depressant, such as inhalants and alcohol, slows the body down.

What Are Inhalants?

From liquid to vapor

Inhalants include many common consumer products. Many products, such as nail polish and paint, are dissolved in **solvents**. They are sold as liquids in airtight containers. When the polish or paint is applied, the solvent quickly **evaporates** into the air. This means that the liquid solvent becomes a **vapor**, and the polish or paint soon dries hard. **Volatile substances**, such as gasoline and **butane**, also evaporate quickly.

Dangerous fumes

Substances that evaporate quickly can easily be **inhaled**. In some industries workers wear masks to protect them from **fumes**. The chemicals in the solvents can damage their lungs and affect their brain. Deliberately breathing the vapor deep into the lungs is inhalant abuse. It is called **sniffing** or **huffing**.

A professional painter uses a mask so that he does not breathe in the vapor from the paint spray. He knows the spray will damage his lungs if he breathes it in.

Aerosols

Many **aerosols** contain solvents, but they also contain another gas. This is the gas that pushes the substance out of the can. It is called the **propellant**. It is very cold and particularly dangerous to inhale, because it can freeze the throat and make the user choke.

All of these products have been used for sniffing. They contain solvents or volatile substances.

7

Inhalant Use and the Law

It is not against the law to sell or to have the more than 1,000 common household products that can be abused by **inhaling**. These products are available at home, in school, and can be bought in stores. Any laws that forbid the sale of these products to young people are difficult to enforce. However, young people who are caught **sniffing** may be taken into the care of local authorities. The best prevention is to educate young people and make them aware that when inhalants get into their bloodstream, it can kill them.

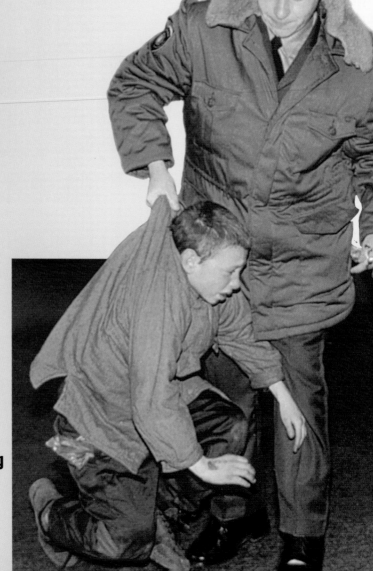

Sniffing can make people rowdy and aggressive. This policeman has stopped this boy because he might be in danger of hurting himself or others.

Who is doing it?

The National Household Survey on Drugs reports that almost as many eighth-graders have abused inhalants as have tried **marijuana**. And among high school students, inhalant abuse is the fourth most commonly abused substance. It follows the abuse of alcohol, tobacco, and marijuana.

What do parents think?

It seems that many parents are not aware that kids are using inhalants at alarming rates. More than nine out of ten parents do not believe that their children may have abused inhalants. Yet one in five students in the United States has used an inhalant to get **high** by the time he or she has reached eighth grade. Adults and kids need to know the facts. Inhalants are not drugs. They are poisonous chemicals.

The right to buy?

What would you do if a store clerk refused to sell you a substance, such as a glue or paint thinner, that contained solvents or volatile substances? Would you try to explain that you were not going to sniff it, or would you accept that the salesperson is only doing his or her job?

Effects on the Body

What happens when people sniff?

When someone breathes in gas from a **solvent**, the **fumes** pass through the nose into the throat and then down the **trachea** into the lungs. The **chemicals** in the fumes pass into the blood and are pumped around the body. The chemicals take effect very quickly. They make the person feel **high**—dizzy and a bit drunk. They also make the person feel sick.

A lack of oxygen

Many of the effects of **sniffing**, such as dizziness and passing out, are due to a lack of oxygen in the body. Normally we breathe in air, which is a mixture of the gases oxygen and nitrogen. The oxygen passes into our blood and keeps all the body's **cells** alive. When someone **inhales** other chemicals, less oxygen gets into the body.

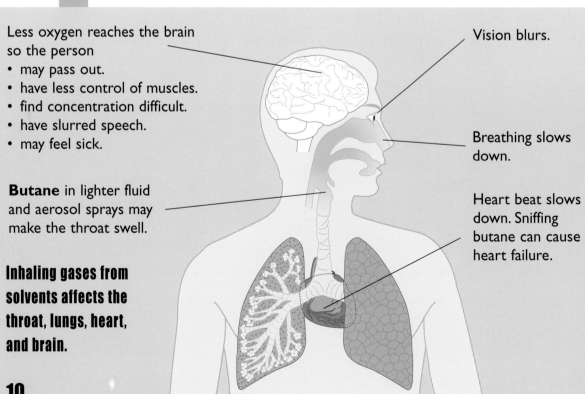

Less oxygen reaches the brain so the person
• may pass out.
• have less control of muscles.
• find concentration difficult.
• have slurred speech.
• may feel sick.

Butane in lighter fluid and aerosol sprays may make the throat swell.

Inhaling gases from solvents affects the throat, lungs, heart, and brain.

Vision blurs.

Breathing slows down.

Heart beat slows down. Sniffing butane can cause heart failure.

The aftereffects

The effects of sniffing only last from 15 to 45 minutes, but the user may be left with a hangover. They may feel moody and have a bad headache. They will also find it difficult to concentrate.

Even a one time abuse of an inhalant can cause hallucinations and loss of feeling in the hands and feet. The lack of oxygen to the brain can cause brain damage. It's also possible that one time use will cause a person to **suffocate** and die.

Inhaling the chemicals in these products can cause death. They can cause breathing to stop or a heart to stop beating. They can cause a person to do careless, life-threatening things.

Effects on the Mind

Fooling around

Most people use inhalants because it makes them feel light-headed and happy. They laugh a lot, even at things that are not really funny. They like to fool around and fall over.

Hidden dangers

Inhalants affect the brain so that the person becomes confused and slower to react to ordinary dangers, such as crossing a road. Their judgment is affected, and they are more likely to have an accident and hurt themselves. **Sniffing** also makes people less inhibited or shy. This means that they are less able to control themselves. Some people shout loudly and become more aggressive when they have been sniffing.

Did you know?

Abusing inhalants affects your school work. Sniffers have lower grades, poorer attendance, and are more likely to be suspended, expelled, or drop out than nonabusers.

Talking point

Neil and his friends say that they inhale inhalants because they are bored. They always go to a special place near a railway station. They like to hear the trains thundering close by because it adds to the feeling of danger. Why do you think people like Neil enjoy the feeling of danger? Do you think they are aware of the real dangers?

Hallucinations

About half of the people who sniff inhalants say they do so because it makes them **hallucinate**. This means that things look unreal to them or that they see things that they know are not really there. They may see cartoon monsters or feel as if they are flying. Hallucinations can be very frightening and may become like a terrifying horror movie.

Many people like to sniff because it can make things seem distorted and unreal. This unreal world can become a nightmare.

Regular Sniffing

An escape

People who **inhale** often have to take larger and larger amounts to get **high**. However, inhalants are not **physically addictive**. This means that an abuser does not need inhalants to feel normal. However, inhalants can become **psychologically addictive**. People who use them are often bored and unhappy. They sniff inhalants to help them escape from their problems. A few people feel that they cannot live without inhalants.

Substance abuse in rural areas and small towns has reached alarming rates.

Lasting damage

Inhalants damage the body, and some inhalants can cause permanent damage. Inhaling **fumes** from **aerosols** and cleaning fluids for several years can damage the kidneys and liver forever. It can cause a lack of bladder control. **Sniffing** can also cause brain damage from which a person will never recover.

Other medical problems

Sniffing can cause a loss of memory and can impair your hearing. It also makes your nose and eyes red and runny. Some people have medical problems that will be made worse by using inhalants. For example, a weakness in the kidneys or heart can be made much worse by regular sniffing.

Inhalants can damage the body in many different ways.

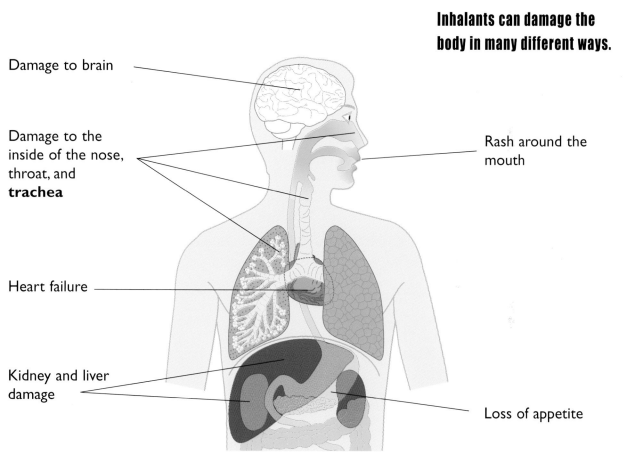

Damage to brain

Damage to the inside of the nose, throat, and **trachea**

Heart failure

Kidney and liver damage

Rash around the mouth

Loss of appetite

Did you know?

The American Academy of Pediatrics warns that abusing inhalants can cause "Sudden Sniffing Death Syndrome." This can occur right after any use of an inhalant. The heart beats rapidly and unevenly and the user dies, having suffered cardiac arrest.

Danger!

Deadly results

Using inhalants can kill you. The most dangerous thing to do is to spray an **aerosol** straight into the mouth and throat. Many aerosols and lighter fluids contain **butane**, which makes the throat swell so the person cannot breathe. As a result, he or she **suffocates**. One of the biggest causes of death is heart attack. Aerosols and butane can make the heart sensitive to shock and excitement.

Death by choking

Inhalants can kill in other ways, too. Many people pass out when they **inhale**. If they are inhaling from a large plastic bag, the bag can stick to their face and suffocate them. If they vomit when they are **unconscious**, the vomit might stick in their throat and choke them, or they may breathe some of the vomit into their lungs and drown.

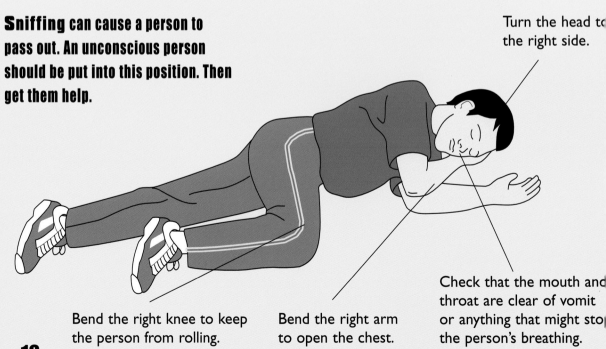

Sniffing can cause a person to pass out. An unconscious person should be put into this position. Then get them help.

Turn the head to the right side.

Bend the right knee to keep the person from rolling.

Bend the right arm to open the chest.

Check that the mouth and throat are clear of vomit or anything that might sto[p] the person's breathing.

Other dangers

People who use inhalants are putting themselves in danger. They have little control over which **chemicals** they are inhaling, and different people react to different amounts of chemicals. Some people become violent. Many users accidentally injure themselves or other people. For example, **solvents**, such as cleaning fluids, burn easily. If users spill solvents on their clothes and light a match, their clothes could burst into flames.

People who abuse inhalants often go to places where they can be alone and will not be noticed by the police or their parents. But this also means that there is no one to help them when things go wrong.

Dealing with an emergency

Would you know what to do if you found someone who was unconscious? Getting help is important, but sometimes immediate help is needed. Do you think that schools should teach basic first aid, or do you think that the emergency services are the best people to cope with a crisis?

Why Do Some People Do It?

Cheap highs

Most people who use inhalants do so because they think that they will like the way it makes them feel. They forget about the dangers. They think it will give them a buzz and that it will be fun.

Inhalants are easy to get hold of because they include many everyday products that are free or inexpensive. There are no **drug dealers** from whom to buy. And there is no special equipment to use. Inhalants may seem to be an easy way to get **high**, but the price to pay, your health and maybe your life, is very, very high.

Curiosity and boredom

Many people **inhale** for the first time out of curiosity. They want to see what it is like, and they only do it once or twice. Other people inhale because they are bored and can't think of anything else to do. If their friends are inhaling, they decide to try it, too. Some people use inhalants because they think it is daring and they like to shock other people. Many older people are alarmed and frightened by the way young people behave when they are high on inhalants.

Young people who are lonely and bored may use inhalants to become part of a group.

Inhaling alone

Some people inhale because they are very unhappy and want to escape from their problems. But they tend to have more emotional problems than nonusers or users of other drugs. They suffer from anxiety, depression, and anger.

Did you know?

The signs that someone is abusing inhalants include:
• paint or stains on their body or clothes
• spots or sores around their mouth
• red or runny eyes or nose
• a chemical smell on their breath
• looking dazed
• sick to their stomach
• anxiety
• excitability
• irritability

Over 100 million children in the world live on the street. Many of them use inhalants. They often do it so that they can stay awake and alert to other dangers, such as street violence. Inhaling also stops them from feeling hungry.

Think about it

Stephen's father is out of work and often drunk and his mother is hardly ever at home. Stephen is bullied by his older brother. He uses inhalants to escape and have some fun, but inhaling soon gets him into trouble at school, so his problems increase. If Stephen was your friend, what would you say to him? Where could he go for help?

Giving Up

Giving up
inhalants can
mean that you
have to find new
friends. Try to
find a group of
friends who
accept you as you
are and don't
simply want you
to be like them.

Giving up inhalants

The good news about giving up inhalants is that
inhalants are not **addictive**. People who are addicted
to alcohol or **heroin** go through a long period of
withdrawal when they stop. But as soon as someone
stops using inhalants, they usually feel better, not worse.

They have fewer headaches, their skin improves, and
they have more energy. Most of the damage to the
nose, throat, and lungs quickly heals. However, if the
person has **inhaled** very poisonous substances, such as
lead, there may be permanent damage. (See pages 14
and 15.) The best advice is, "Don't even do it once!"

Mental addiction

Using inhalants can be **psychologically addictive** for some people. When they stop abusing the **chemicals**, they miss the excitement and the **high**. Most people who use inhalants regularly do so because of other problems in their lives. When they stop using inhalants, the problems are still there. They may need help to solve them.

Did you know?

Spraying **aerosols** straight into the mouth is one of the most dangerous ways to inhale. Apart from possibly causing heart failure, the spray contains other things, such as solid particles of paint or lacquer, which can coat the throat and clog the lungs.

The body does not need inhalants, and the person feels physically better without them.

Saying No

What would you do if someone wanted you to use inhalants with them? Many children are worried that if they say no, people will think they are scared or childish. However, it is dangerous to use inhalants. It's not worth taking risks just to appear cool.

You don't have to give an excuse for saying no. Just say very clearly that you don't want to do it. People are more likely to leave you alone if they know you have made up your mind.

The best thing that you can do for yourself is to know the facts. Inhalants are chemicals which were never intended to be **inhaled** into the human body. Remember, using inhalants, even one time, can kill you.

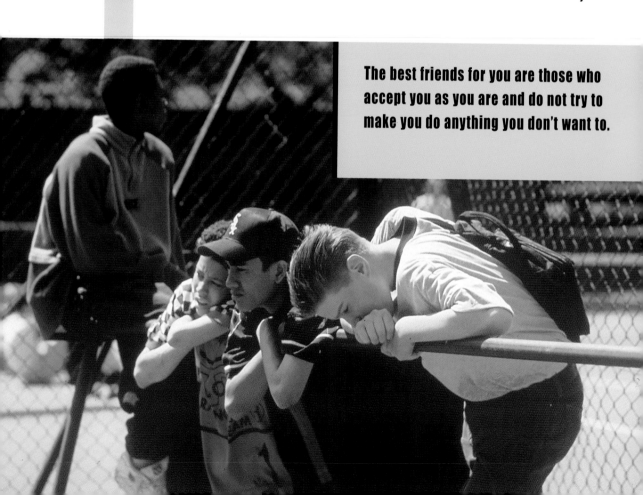

The best friends for you are those who accept you as you are and do not try to make you do anything you don't want to.

Best friends

As you grow up, you become more independent of your family. Being in a group with your friends can then seem very important. But if your friends are experimenting with inhalants or other things that you don't want to do, then you should think about whether they are the right friends for you. Choose friends you like and who have the same interests as you.

When you exercise, your brain releases natural **chemicals** that make you feel good. Playing sports and exercising will make you feel much better than inhalants or drugs.

What do I say?

If friends tried to persuade you to use inhalants what would you say to them? What information about the danger of inhalants would you share with them?

Did you know?

Experimenting with inhalants is done by both boys and girls. However, long-term use is more common with boys. This is probably why more boys than girls die from inhalant use.

Avoiding Difficult Situations

Many young people like to spend time with their friends after school. But if you think your friends are planning to use inhalants, it is better not to go with them than to go and then try to avoid **sniffing**. Avoid any situation where kids might be abusing inhalants.

Dangerous places

Be particularly wary if your friends go to an isolated place to use inhalants or to a park or somewhere that is dangerous after dark. Many **drug dealers** and **addicts** use such places, too. If anything goes wrong, it is much harder to get help fast.

People who sniff or **huff** often skip classes. As a result, they don't just miss school work—they usually end up being bored and getting into trouble.

Truancy

People who regularly do inhalants often skip school and get involved in vandalism or fights. Hanging out with friends who are inhaling, even if you do not **inhale** yourself, means that you are also going to get involved in trouble.

How do you know?

Someone you know may be abusing inhalants if they

· constantly smell the sleeves of their clothing.
· sniff marking pens.
· hide rags or empty containers in closets or lockers.

What should you do if you suspect inhalant abuse?

Most schools have after-school activities in which you can take part. You might make new friends, too.

Dealing with Stress

Good and bad times

Growing up is an exciting and enjoyable time. You can try new things and begin to make decisions for yourself. It can also be a difficult time. There are important tests to study for. Friendships don't always run smoothly. Most kids worry about the way they look, whether people will like them, and what they are going to do with their lives.

Time to relax

When you are under stress, it is important to make time to relax and enjoy yourself. It is a good idea to take time to do some physical exercise and relax your mind. Exercise helps to make you feel good.

Talking over a problem can help you feel better or help you to find a solution. If you can't talk to a friend or someone in your family, talk to an adult you can trust, such as a teacher.

Getting help

Some young people have serious problems at home or at school. Using inhalants may help them to escape from their problems, but only for a short time. When the effect wears off, the problems are still there, and they feel tired and ill as well.

It is better to face up to problems and try to sort them out. If you have problems that you feel you cannot deal with, don't despair. Ask for help. There are people and organizations who can help you. If you can, ask for help from your family, your friends, or your teachers. If at first people don't listen to you, go on looking and asking for help until you get it.

Sometimes talking on the telephone is easier than talking to someone face to face. If you need help, but can't talk to any of the people you know, then you can call the National Inhalant Prevention Partnership.

Did you know?

If you want to talk to someone about inhalants, you can call the National Inhalant Prevention Partnership. The number is 800/ 269-4237. The counselor you talk to will be able to tell you where you can go in your neighborhood to get help.

Talk it over

When you are unhappy it is easy to think that things will never change for the better. How would you persuade someone to get help with their problems?

Preventing Inhalant Abuse

Safer sprays
Sniffing aerosols is the most dangerous form of inhaling. Some people asked manufacturers to add an unpleasant smell to aerosols. The manufacturers refused because no one would want to buy hairspray or deodorant that smelled terrible. However, many products that are sold as aerosols could be changed to spray bottles that work without a dangerous aerosol **propellant**.

Beating boredom
Another way to prevent people using inhalants is to look at the reasons why they do it. Young people often feel bored and angry. They need to have places to go where they can do interesting and exciting things, such as acting in a play, performing in a band, or learning how to rock climb. Activities like these can help young people to feel more confident, happy, and secure.

Many products can be sold as sprays that do not contain inhalants.

Know the facts

So many common products contain inhalants that it is impossible to keep them all out of reach. So preteens and teens need to be smart about the facts. Inhaling deadly chemicals and poisons puts your health, eduction, and relationships with family and friends at great risk. Inhaling just one time could make you do something that you will regret for the rest of your life. Inhaling just one time can kill you.

Young people who have nowhere to go and nothing to do are at risk to be inhalant abusers. They need places, like this recreational center, where they can meet others and have a good, safe time.

Should the government take action?

What do you think the government should do to stop people abusing inhalants? Think about how much money each of your suggestions would cost.

Useful Contacts

Inhalants

National Inhalant Prevention Partnership – provides free support and information about how to stop using inhalants:
telephone: 800/ 269-4337.

Other Problems

Covenant House – offers confidential support and help for children worried about problems with friends, family, drugs, and alcohol:
telephone: 800/ 999-9999.

Drug and Alcohol Abuse Hotline – talk to a counselor about drug and alcohol problems:
telephone: 800/ 729-6686.

Spanish Hotline – talk to a counselor in spanish:
telephone: 800/ 344-7432.

More Books to Read

Chier, Ruth. *Danger: Inhalants.*New York: Rosen Publishing Co.,1996.

Desmond, Theresa and Paul Almonte. *Drug Use and Abuse.* Parsippanny, N. J.: Silver Burdet Press, 1995.

Jaffe, Steven L. *How to Get Help.* Broomal, Penn.: Chelsea House Publishers, 1999.

Sanders, Pete, and Steve Myers. *Drugs.* Brookfield, Conn.: Millbrook Press, Inc. 1996.

Glossary

addict someone who cannot give up a habit, such as smoking cigarettes or taking heroin

addictive causing someone to form a habit they cannot give up

aerosol can containing a liquid that is released as a fine spray

asthma tightening of the tubes in the lungs, which makes breathing difficult

butane gas burned as a fuel

cells building blocks of all living things, including the human body

chemical substance that is used in chemistry

depressant substance that slows down the body's reactions and relaxes the muscles

drug dealer someone who sells or deals in drugs

Ecstasy illegal stimulant

evaporate turn from a liquid into a gas

fumes unpleasant or poisonous gases or smoke

hallucinate to experience things that are imagined as if they are real

hallucinogen substance that causes a person to hallucinate

heroin an addictive, illegal drug made from a particular kind of poppy

high drunk or exhilarated by drugs

huffing dangerous deliberate breathing in of common products in order to get high

illegal drug drug, such as heroin, LSD, or marijuana, that is forbidden by law

inhale breathe in

legal drug substance that affects the body but is allowed by law. Medicines, coffee, and tea are legal drugs.

LSD an illegal, powerful hallucinogen

marijuana an illegal drug made from hemp. Marijuana is also called cannabis and hashish.

medicine substance used to treat or cure illnesses

physically addictive causing the body to be unable to work normally without a particular substance, such as nicotine in tobacco, or heroin

prescribe give a medicine under the advice or order of a doctor

propellant gas used in an aerosol to push a fine spray of the contents out of the can

psychologically addictive causing a person's behavior to become dependent on using a particular substance. The person feels they cannot manage without it.

sniffing dangerous deliberate breathing in of common products in order to get high

solvent a liquid in which another substance is dissolved

stimulant ubstance that speeds up the body

suffocate make unable to breathe

trachea air carrying tube of the respiratory system; windpipe

unconscious unaware of what is happening

vapor gas

volatile substance substance that evaporates easily

withdrawal taking away, especially of an addictive drug. Withdrawal symptoms include craving and physically unpleasant feelings that are experienced until the body gets used to managing without the drug.

31

Index

accidents 12, 17
addiction 14, 20, 21
aerosols 7, 10, 14, 16,
    21, 28
aggression 8, 12, 17
asthma 4
brain 10, 11, 14, 15
butane 6, 10, 16
chemicals 10, 17
cleaning fluids 14
crime 8, 9
curiosity 18
deaths 11, 16, 17, 25, 29
depressant 5
driving 8
excuses 22
exercise 23
friends 22, 23, 24, 25, 26
giving up 20–21
hallucinogen 5, 13
heart 5, 10, 15, 29
illegal drugs 4, 5
kidneys 14, 15
legal drugs 4
lighter fluid 5, 7, 10
light-headedness 12
liver 14, 15
lungs 10, 20, 21
medicines 4
oxygen 10

passing out see
    unconscious
plastic bags 16, 29
police 8
propellant 7
recovery position 16
solvent 7, 9, 10
stimulant 5
store clerks 9
street children 19
stress 26, 27
suffocation 11, 16
throat 10, 15, 16, 20,
    21, 29
truancy 24, 25
unconscious 10, 16, 17
vapor 6
vandalism 25
volatile substances 6
vomit 16, 29